Self Care
PLANNER

NAME:

Take care of yourself first

Date : _____   Today's goal: _____

Wake up time : _____   _____

Hours of sleep : _____   _____

_____

What am I gratful for today	To do list

Meals

Breakfast	Lunch	Dinner	Snacks
Kcal	Kcal	Kcal	Kcal

Water intake	🥛 🥛 🥛 🥛 🥛 🥛 🥛 🥛 🥛 🥛

Today's exercise

My Mood Today   ☹ 🙁 🙂 😊 😃

Note

_____
_____
_____
_____
_____

A moment to remember

What I learnt today

Things that made me smile

Habits

Positive affirmation

Tomorrow's will

Date   : _____   Today's goal: _____

Wake up time : _____   _____

Hours of sleep : _____   _____

                                         _____

What am I gratful for today	To do list

Meals

Breakfast	Lunch	Dinner	Snacks
Kcal	Kcal	Kcal	Kcal

Water intake	🥛 🥛 🥛 🥛 🥛 🥛 🥛 🥛 🥛 🥛

Today's exercise

My Mood Today   ☹ 🙁 🙂 😊 😀

Note

_____

_____

_____

_____

A moment to remember

What I learnt today

Things that made me smile

Habits

Positive affirmation

Tomorrow's will

Date : _____   Today's goal: _____
Wake up time : _____   _____
Hours of sleep : _____   _____
_____

What am I gratful for today	To do list

Meals

Breakfast	Lunch	Dinner	Snacks
Kcal	Kcal	Kcal	Kcal

Water intake 🥛 🥛 🥛 🥛 🥛 🥛 🥛 🥛 🥛 🥛

Today's exercise

My Mood Today   ☹ 🙁 🙂 😊 😃

Note

_____
_____
_____
_____

A moment to remember

What I learnt today

Things that made me smile

Habits

Positive affirmation

Tomorrow's will

Date : _____   Today's goal: _____

Wake up time : _____   _____

Hours of sleep : _____   _____

_____

What am I gratful for today	To do list

Meals

Breakfast	Lunch	Dinner	Snacks
Kcal	Kcal	Kcal	Kcal

Water intake	🥛 🥛 🥛 🥛 🥛 🥛 🥛 🥛 🥛 🥛

Today's exercise

My Mood Today   ☹️ 🙁 🙂 😊 😃

Note

_____

_____

_____

_____

_____

A moment to remember

What I learnt today

Things that made me smile

Habits

Positive affirmation

Tomorrow's will

Date : _____   Today's goal: _____
Wake up time : _____   _____
Hours of sleep : _____   _____
_____

What am I gratful for today	To do list

Meals

Breakfast	Lunch	Dinner	Snacks
Kcal	Kcal	Kcal	Kcal

Water intake ☐ ☐ ☐ ☐ ☐ ☐ ☐ ☐ ☐ ☐

Today's exercise

My Mood Today   ☹ ☹ ☺ ☺ 😄

Note

_____
_____
_____
_____
_____
_____

A moment to remember

What I learnt today

Things that made me smile

Habits

Positive affirmation

Tomorrow's will

Date   : _____   Today's goal: _____

Wake up time : _____   _____

Hours of sleep : _____   _____

_____

What am I gratful for today	To do list

Meals

Breakfast	Lunch	Dinner	Snacks
Kcal	Kcal	Kcal	Kcal

Water intake	🥛 🥛 🥛 🥛 🥛 🥛 🥛 🥛 🥛 🥛

Today's exercise

My Mood Today   ☹ 🙁 🙂 😊 😀

Note

_____
_____
_____
_____

A moment to remember

What I learnt today

Things that made me smile

Habits

Positive affirmation

Tomorrow's will

Date : _____ Today's goal: _____

Wake up time : _____ _____

Hours of sleep : _____ _____

_____

What am I gratful for today	To do list

Meals

Breakfast	Lunch	Dinner	Snacks
Kcal	Kcal	Kcal	Kcal
Water intake			

Today's exercise

My Mood Today ☹ 🙁 😊 🙂 😀

Note

_____

_____

_____

_____

_____

A moment to remember

What I learnt today

Things that made me smile

Habits

Positive affirmation

Tomorrow's will

Date : _____   Today's goal: _____

Wake up time : _____   _____

Hours of sleep : _____   _____

_____

What am I gratful for today	To do list

Meals

Breakfast	Lunch	Dinner	Snacks
Kcal	Kcal	Kcal	Kcal

Water intake	🥛 🥛 🥛 🥛 🥛 🥛 🥛 🥛 🥛 🥛

Today's exercise

My Mood Today   ☹️ 🙁 🙂 😊 😀

Note

_____

_____

_____

_____

_____

A moment to remember

What I learnt today

Things that made me smile

Habits

Positive affirmation

Tomorrow's will

Date   : _____   Today's goal: _____

Wake up time : _____   _____

Hours of sleep : _____   _____

_____

What am I gratful for today	To do list

Meals

Breakfast	Lunch	Dinner	Snacks
Kcal	Kcal	Kcal	Kcal

Water intake	

Today's exercise

My Mood Today

Note

_____
_____
_____
_____

A moment to remember

What I learnt today

Things that made me smile

Habits

Positive affirmation

Tomorrow's will

Date : _____   Today's goal: _____

Wake up time : _____   _____

Hours of sleep : _____   _____

_____

What am I gratful for today	To do list

Meals

Breakfast	Lunch	Dinner	Snacks
Kcal	Kcal	Kcal	Kcal

Water intake	🥛 🥛 🥛 🥛 🥛 🥛 🥛 🥛 🥛 🥛

Today's exercise

My Mood Today   ☹ 🙁 🙂 😊 😃

Note

_____
_____
_____
_____
_____

A moment to remember

What I learnt today

Things that made me smile

Habits

Positive affirmation

Tomorrow's will

Date   : _____   Today's goal: _____
Wake up time : _____   _____
Hours of sleep : _____   _____
                                                              _____

What am I gratful for today	To do list

Meals

Breakfast	Lunch	Dinner	Snacks
Kcal	Kcal	Kcal	Kcal

Water intake | 🥛 🥛 🥛 🥛 🥛 🥛 🥛 🥛 🥛 🥛

Today's exercise

My Mood Today   ☹ 🙁 🙂 😊 😃

Note

_____
_____
_____
_____
_____

A moment to remember

What I learnt today

Things that made me smile

Habits

Positive affirmation

Tomorrow's will

Date : _____ Today's goal: _____

Wake up time : _____ _____

Hours of sleep : _____ _____

_____

What am I gratful for today	To do list

Meals

Breakfast	Lunch	Dinner	Snacks
Kcal	Kcal	Kcal	Kcal

Water intake	⬜ ⬜ ⬜ ⬜ ⬜ ⬜ ⬜ ⬜ ⬜ ⬜

Today's exercise

My Mood Today   ☹ 🙁 🙂 😊 😃

Note

_____

_____

_____

_____

A moment to remember

What I learnt today

Things that made me smile

Habits

Positive affirmation

Tomorrow's will

Date : _____ Today's goal: _____

Wake up time : _____ _____

Hours of sleep : _____ _____

_____

What am I gratful for today	To do list

Meals

Breakfast	Lunch	Dinner	Snacks
Kcal	Kcal	Kcal	Kcal
Water intake	🥛 🥛 🥛 🥛 🥛 🥛 🥛 🥛 🥛 🥛		

Today's exercise

My Mood Today 😠 😟 🙂 😊 😃

Note

_____
_____
_____
_____

A moment to remember

What I learnt today

Things that made me smile

Habits

Positive affirmation

Tomorrow's will

Date : _____

Wake up time : _____

Hours of sleep : _____

Today's goal: _____
_____
_____
_____

What am I gratful for today

To do list

Meals

Breakfast	Lunch	Dinner	Snacks
Kcal	Kcal	Kcal	Kcal

Water intake	🥛 🥛 🥛 🥛 🥛 🥛 🥛 🥛 🥛 🥛

Today's exercise

My Mood Today   ☹ 🙁 🙂 😊 😀

Note

_____
_____
_____
_____
_____

A moment to remember

What I learnt today

Things that made me smile

Habits

Positive affirmation

Tomorrow's will

Date : _____   Today's goal: _____

Wake up time : _____   _____

Hours of sleep : _____   _____

_____

What am I gratful for today	To do list

Meals

Breakfast	Lunch	Dinner	Snacks
Kcal	Kcal	Kcal	Kcal

Water intake	🥛 🥛 🥛 🥛 🥛 🥛 🥛 🥛 🥛 🥛

Today's exercise

My Mood Today   ☹ 🙁 🙂 😊 😄

Note

_____

_____

_____

_____

_____

A moment to remember

What I learnt today

Things that made me smile

Habits

Positive affirmation

Tomorrow's will

Date : _____   Today's goal: _____

Wake up time : _____   _____

Hours of sleep : _____   _____

_____

What am I gratful for today

To do list

Meals

Breakfast	Lunch	Dinner	Snacks
Kcal	Kcal	Kcal	Kcal

Water intake	

Today's exercise

My Mood Today   ☹ ☹ ☺ ☺ 😀

Note

_____
_____
_____
_____
_____

A moment to remember

What I learnt today

Things that made me smile

Habits

Positive affirmation

Tomorrow's will

Date : _____   Today's goal: _____
Wake up time : _____   _____
Hours of sleep : _____   _____
_____

What am I gratful for today	To do list

Meals

Breakfast	Lunch	Dinner	Snacks
Kcal	Kcal	Kcal	Kcal

Water intake   ▯ ▯ ▯ ▯ ▯ ▯ ▯ ▯ ▯ ▯

Today's exercise

My Mood Today   ☹ 🙁 🙂 😊 😃

Note

_____
_____
_____
_____

A moment to remember

What I learnt today

Things that made me smile

Habits

Positive affirmation

Tomorrow's will

Date   : _____   Today's goal: _____

Wake up time : _____   _____

Hours of sleep : _____   _____

What am I gratful for today	To do list

Meals

Breakfast	Lunch	Dinner	Snacks
Kcal	Kcal	Kcal	Kcal

Water intake	🥛 🥛 🥛 🥛 🥛 🥛 🥛 🥛 🥛 🥛

Today's exercise

My Mood Today   ☹ 🙁 🙂 😊 😃

Note

_____

_____

_____

_____

_____

A moment to remember

What I learnt today

Things that made me smile

Habits

Positive affirmation

Tomorrow's will

Date : _____   Today's goal: _____

Wake up time : _____   _____

Hours of sleep : _____ _____

What am I gratful for today	To do list

Meals

Breakfast	Lunch	Dinner	Snacks
Kcal	Kcal	Kcal	Kcal
Water intake	☐ ☐ ☐ ☐ ☐ ☐ ☐ ☐ ☐ ☐		

Today's exercise

My Mood Today   ☹ ☹ ☺ ☺ ☺

Note

_____

_____

_____

_____

A moment to remember

What I learnt today

Things that made me smile

Habits

Positive affirmation

Tomorrow's will

Date : _____   Today's goal: _____

Wake up time : _____   _____

Hours of sleep : _____   _____

_____

What am I gratful for today	To do list

Meals

Breakfast	Lunch	Dinner	Snacks
Kcal	Kcal	Kcal	Kcal

Water intake	🥛 🥛 🥛 🥛 🥛 🥛 🥛 🥛 🥛 🥛

Today's exercise

My Mood Today   ☹ ☹ 🙂 🙂 😃

Note

_____

_____

_____

_____

A moment to remember

What I learnt today

Things that made me smile

Habits

Positive affirmation

Tomorrow's will

Date   : _____   Today's goal: _____

Wake up time : _____   _____

Hours of sleep : _____   _____

_____

What am I gratful for today	To do list

Meals

Breakfast	Lunch	Dinner	Snacks
Kcal	Kcal	Kcal	Kcal

Water intake	□ □ □ □ □ □ □ □ □ □

Today's exercise

My Mood Today   ☹ ☹ ☺ ☺ ☺

Note

_____
_____
_____
_____
_____

A moment to remember

What I learnt today

Things that made me smile

Habits

Positive affirmation

Tomorrow's will

Date   : _____   Today's goal: _____

Wake up time : _____   _____

Hours of sleep : _____   _____

_____

What am I gratful for today	To do list

Meals

Breakfast	Lunch	Dinner	Snacks
Kcal	Kcal	Kcal	Kcal
Water intake	☐ ☐ ☐ ☐ ☐ ☐ ☐ ☐ ☐ ☐		

Today's exercise

My Mood Today   ☹ ☹ ☺ ☺ ☺

Note

_____

_____

_____

_____

A moment to remember

What I learnt today

Things that made me smile

Habits

Positive affirmation

Tomorrow's will

Date : _____   Today's goal: _____

Wake up time : _____   _____

Hours of sleep : _____   _____

What am I gratful for today	To do list

Meals

Breakfast	Lunch	Dinner	Snacks
Kcal	Kcal	Kcal	Kcal

Water intake   ☐ ☐ ☐ ☐ ☐ ☐ ☐ ☐ ☐ ☐

Today's exercise

My Mood Today   ☹ 🙁 🙂 😊 😀

Note

_____

_____

_____

_____

A moment to remember

What I learnt today

Things that made me smile

Habits

Positive affirmation

Tomorrow's will

Date : _____   Today's goal: _____

Wake up time : _____   _____

Hours of sleep : _____   _____

What am I gratful for today	To do list

Meals

Breakfast	Lunch	Dinner	Snacks
Kcal	Kcal	Kcal	Kcal

Water intake	☐ ☐ ☐ ☐ ☐ ☐ ☐ ☐ ☐ ☐

Today's exercise

My Mood Today   ☹ ☹ ☺ ☺ ☺

Note

_____
_____
_____
_____
_____

A moment to remember

What I learnt today

Things that made me smile

Habits

Positive affirmation

Tomorrow's will

Date : _____   Today's goal: _____
Wake up time : _____   _____
Hours of sleep : _____   _____
_____

What am I gratful for today	To do list

Meals

Breakfast	Lunch	Dinner	Snacks
Kcal	Kcal	Kcal	Kcal

Water intake ▢ ▢ ▢ ▢ ▢ ▢ ▢ ▢ ▢ ▢

Today's exercise

My Mood Today   ☹ ☹ ☺ ☺ ☺

Note

_____
_____
_____
_____
_____

A moment to remember

What I learnt today

Things that made me smile

Habits

Positive affirmation

Tomorrow's will

Date : _____   Today's goal: _____

Wake up time : _____   _____

Hours of sleep : _____   _____

What am I gratful for today	To do list

Meals

Breakfast	Lunch	Dinner	Snacks
Kcal	Kcal	Kcal	Kcal
Water intake			

Today's exercise

My Mood Today   ☹ 🙁 🙂 😊 😃

Note

_____
_____
_____
_____
_____

A moment to remember

What I learnt today

Things that made me smile

Habits

Positive affirmation

Tomorrow's will

Date : _____   Today's goal: _____

Wake up time : _____   _____

Hours of sleep : _____   _____

_____

What am I gratful for today	To do list

Meals

Breakfast	Lunch	Dinner	Snacks
Kcal	Kcal	Kcal	Kcal
Water intake			

Today's exercise

My Mood Today   😠 😟 🙂 ☺ 😄

Note

_____

_____

_____

_____

_____

A moment to remember

What I learnt today

Things that made me smile

Habits

Positive affirmation

Tomorrow's will

Date   : _____   Today's goal: _____

Wake up time : _____   _____

Hours of sleep : _____   _____

What am I gratful for today	To do list

Meals

Breakfast	Lunch	Dinner	Snacks
Kcal	Kcal	Kcal	Kcal

Water intake	🥛 🥛 🥛 🥛 🥛 🥛 🥛 🥛 🥛 🥛

Today's exercise

My Mood Today   ☹ 🙁 🙂 😊 😃

Note

_____

_____

_____

_____

A moment to remember

What I learnt today

Things that made me smile

Habits

Positive affirmation

Tomorrow's will

Date : _____   Today's goal: _____

Wake up time : _____   _____

Hours of sleep : _____   _____

_____

What am I gratful for today	To do list

Meals

Breakfast	Lunch	Dinner	Snacks
Kcal	Kcal	Kcal	Kcal

Water intake	🥛 🥛 🥛 🥛 🥛 🥛 🥛 🥛 🥛 🥛

Today's exercise

My Mood Today   ☹ 🙁 🙂 😊 😃

Note

_____

_____

_____

_____

_____

A moment to remember

What I learnt today

Things that made me smile

Habits

Positive affirmation

Tomorrow's will

Date   : _____   Today's goal: _____

Wake up time : _____   _____

Hours of sleep : _____   _____

What am I gratful for today	To do list

Meals

Breakfast	Lunch	Dinner	Snacks
Kcal	Kcal	Kcal	Kcal
Water intake	▢ ▢ ▢ ▢ ▢ ▢ ▢ ▢ ▢ ▢		

Today's exercise

My Mood Today   ☹ 🙁 🙂 😊 😄

Note

_____
_____
_____
_____

A moment to remember

What I learnt today

Things that made me smile

Habits

Positive affirmation

Tomorrow's will

Date : _____   Today's goal: _____
Wake up time : _____   _____
Hours of sleep : _____   _____
_____

What am I gratful for today	To do list

Meals

Breakfast	Lunch	Dinner	Snacks
Kcal	Kcal	Kcal	Kcal
Water intake	🥛 🥛 🥛 🥛 🥛 🥛 🥛 🥛 🥛 🥛		

Today's exercise

My Mood Today   😠 😟 🙂 😊 😃

Note

_____
_____
_____
_____
_____

A moment to remember

What I learnt today

Things that made me smile

Habits

Positive affirmation

Tomorrow's will

Date   : _____   Today's goal: _____

Wake up time : _____   _____

Hours of sleep : _____   _____

_____

What am I gratful for today	To do list

Meals

Breakfast	Lunch	Dinner	Snacks
Kcal	Kcal	Kcal	Kcal

Water intake	

Today's exercise

My Mood Today   ☹ ☹ ☺ ☺ ☺

Note

_____
_____
_____
_____
_____

A moment to remember

What I learnt today

Things that made me smile

Habits

Positive affirmation

Tomorrow's will

Date : _____   Today's goal: _____
Wake up time : _____   _____
Hours of sleep : _____   _____
_____

What am I gratful for today	To do list

Meals

Breakfast	Lunch	Dinner	Snacks
Kcal	Kcal	Kcal	Kcal

Water intake

Today's exercise

My Mood Today   ☹ 🙁 🙂 😊 😃

Note

_____
_____
_____
_____

A moment to remember

What I learnt today

Things that made me smile

Habits

Positive affirmation

Tomorrow's will

Date : _____   Today's goal: _____

Wake up time : _____   _____

Hours of sleep : _____   _____

What am I gratful for today	To do list

Meals

Breakfast	Lunch	Dinner	Snacks
Kcal	Kcal	Kcal	Kcal
Water intake	🥛 🥛 🥛 🥛 🥛 🥛 🥛 🥛 🥛 🥛		

Today's exercise

My Mood Today   ☹ 🙁 🙂 😊 😃

Note

_____
_____
_____
_____
_____

A moment to remember

What I learnt today

Things that made me smile

Habits

Positive affirmation

Tomorrow's will

Date   : _____   Today's goal: _____

Wake up time : _____   _____

Hours of sleep : _____   _____

_____

What am I gratful for today	To do list

Meals

Breakfast	Lunch	Dinner	Snacks
Kcal	Kcal	Kcal	Kcal

Water intake ⊔ ⊔ ⊔ ⊔ ⊔ ⊔ ⊔ ⊔ ⊔ ⊔

Today's exercise

My Mood Today   ☹ 🙁 🙂 😊 😄

Note

_____

_____

_____

_____

A moment to remember

What I learnt today

Things that made me smile

Habits

Positive affirmation

Tomorrow's will

Date : _____   Today's goal: _____

Wake up time : _____   _____

Hours of sleep : _____   _____

What am I gratful for today	To do list

Meals

Breakfast	Lunch	Dinner	Snacks
Kcal	Kcal	Kcal	Kcal

Water intake ☐ ☐ ☐ ☐ ☐ ☐ ☐ ☐ ☐ ☐

Today's exercise

My Mood Today   ☹ ☹ ☺ ☺ ☺

Note

_____

_____

_____

_____

A moment to remember

What I learnt today

Things that made me smile

Habits

Positive affirmation

Tomorrow's will

Date : _____   Today's goal: _____

Wake up time : _____   _____

Hours of sleep : _____   _____

What am I gratful for today	To do list

Meals

Breakfast	Lunch	Dinner	Snacks
Kcal	Kcal	Kcal	Kcal

Water intake

Today's exercise

My Mood Today

Note

_____
_____
_____
_____

A moment to remember

What I learnt today

Things that made me smile

Habits

Positive affirmation

Tomorrow's will

Date : _____

Wake up time : _____

Hours of sleep : _____

Today's goal: _____
_____
_____

What am I gratful for today

To do list

Meals

Breakfast	Lunch	Dinner	Snacks
Kcal	Kcal	Kcal	Kcal

Water intake	☐ ☐ ☐ ☐ ☐ ☐ ☐ ☐ ☐ ☐

Today's exercise

My Mood Today ☹ ☹ ☺ ☺ ☺

Note

_____
_____
_____
_____

A moment to remember

What I learnt today

Things that made me smile

Habits

Positive affirmation

Tomorrow's will

Date : _____   Today's goal: _____

Wake up time : _____   _____

Hours of sleep : _____   _____

_____

What am I gratful for today	To do list

Meals

Breakfast	Lunch	Dinner	Snacks
Kcal	Kcal	Kcal	Kcal

Water intake

Today's exercise

My Mood Today   😣 😟 🙂 😊 😃

Note

_____

_____

_____

_____

_____

A moment to remember

What I learnt today

Things that made me smile

Habits

Positive affirmation

Tomorrow's will

Date : _____   Today's goal: _____
Wake up time : _____   _____
Hours of sleep : _____   _____
                                        _____

What am I gratful for today	To do list

Meals

Breakfast	Lunch	Dinner	Snacks
Kcal	Kcal	Kcal	Kcal

Water intake ▢ ▢ ▢ ▢ ▢ ▢ ▢ ▢ ▢ ▢

Today's exercise

My Mood Today   ☹ ☹ ☺ ☺ ☺

Note

_____
_____
_____
_____
_____

A moment to remember

What I learnt today

Things that made me smile

Habits

Positive affirmation

Tomorrow's will

Date : _____   Today's goal: _____

Wake up time : _____   _____

Hours of sleep : _____   _____

What am I gratful for today	To do list

Meals

Breakfast	Lunch	Dinner	Snacks
Kcal	Kcal	Kcal	Kcal

Water intake	🥛 🥛 🥛 🥛 🥛 🥛 🥛 🥛 🥛 🥛

Today's exercise

My Mood Today   ☹ 🙁 🙂 😊 😃

Note

_____

_____

_____

_____

_____

A moment to remember

What I learnt today

Things that made me smile

Habits

Positive affirmation

Tomorrow's will

Date : _____   Today's goal: _____

Wake up time : _____   _____

Hours of sleep : _____   _____

What am I gratful for today	To do list

Meals

Breakfast	Lunch	Dinner	Snacks
Kcal	Kcal	Kcal	Kcal

Water intake ▢ ▢ ▢ ▢ ▢ ▢ ▢ ▢ ▢ ▢

Today's exercise

My Mood Today ☹ ☹ ☺ ☺ ☺

Note

_____
_____
_____
_____

A moment to remember

What I learnt today

Things that made me smile

Habits

Positive affirmation

Tomorrow's will

Date : _____   Today's goal: _____
Wake up time : _____   _____
Hours of sleep : _____   _____
_____

What am I gratful for today	To do list

Meals

Breakfast	Lunch	Dinner	Snacks
Kcal	Kcal	Kcal	Kcal

Water intake 🥛 🥛 🥛 🥛 🥛 🥛 🥛 🥛 🥛 🥛

Today's exercise

My Mood Today   ☹ 🙁 🙂 😊 😃

Note

_____
_____
_____
_____

A moment to remember

What I learnt today

Things that made me smile

Habits

Positive affirmation

Tomorrow's will

Date : _____ Today's goal: _____
Wake up time : _____ _____
Hours of sleep : _____ _____

What am I gratful for today	To do list

Meals

Breakfast	Lunch	Dinner	Snacks
Kcal	Kcal	Kcal	Kcal

Water intake	🥛 🥛 🥛 🥛 🥛 🥛 🥛 🥛 🥛 🥛

Today's exercise

My Mood Today   ☹ 🙁 🙂 😊 😄

Note

_____
_____
_____
_____
_____

A moment to remember

What I learnt today

Things that made me smile

Habits

Positive affirmation

Tomorrow's will

Date : _____ Today's goal: _____

Wake up time : _____ _____

Hours of sleep : _____ _____

_____

What am I gratful for today

To do list

Meals

Breakfast	Lunch	Dinner	Snacks
Kcal	Kcal	Kcal	Kcal

Water intake	🥛 🥛 🥛 🥛 🥛 🥛 🥛 🥛 🥛 🥛

Today's exercise

My Mood Today   😣 😟 🙂 😊 😀

Note

_____

_____

_____

_____

A moment to remember

What I learnt today

Things that made me smile

Habits

Positive affirmation

Tomorrow's will

Date : _____   Today's goal: _____
Wake up time : _____   _____
Hours of sleep : _____   _____

What am I gratful for today	To do list

Meals

Breakfast	Lunch	Dinner	Snacks
Kcal	Kcal	Kcal	Kcal

Water intake	🥛 🥛 🥛 🥛 🥛 🥛 🥛 🥛 🥛 🥛

Today's exercise

My Mood Today   ☹️ 🙁 🙂 😊 😃

Note

_____
_____
_____
_____

A moment to remember

What I learnt today

Things that made me smile

Habits

Positive affirmation

Tomorrow's will

Date : _____   Today's goal: _____
Wake up time : _____   _____
Hours of sleep : _____   _____
_____

What am I gratful for today

To do list

Meals

Breakfast	Lunch	Dinner	Snacks
Kcal	Kcal	Kcal	Kcal

Water intake

Today's exercise

My Mood Today   ☹ 🙁 🙂 😊 😃

Note

_____
_____
_____
_____

A moment to remember

What I learnt today

Things that made me smile

Habits

Positive affirmation

Tomorrow's will

Date : _____   Today's goal: _____
Wake up time : _____   _____
Hours of sleep : _____   _____
_____

What am I gratful for today	To do list

Meals

Breakfast	Lunch	Dinner	Snacks
Kcal	Kcal	Kcal	Kcal

Water intake ☐ ☐ ☐ ☐ ☐ ☐ ☐ ☐ ☐ ☐

Today's exercise

My Mood Today   ☹ 🙁 🙂 😊 😃

Note

_____
_____
_____
_____

A moment to remember

What I learnt today

Things that made me smile

Habits

Positive affirmation

Tomorrow's will

Date   : _____   Today's goal: _____

Wake up time : _____   _____

Hours of sleep : _____   _____

                                                              _____

What am I gratful for today	To do list

Meals

Breakfast	Lunch	Dinner	Snacks
Kcal	Kcal	Kcal	Kcal

Water intake	☐ ☐ ☐ ☐ ☐ ☐ ☐ ☐ ☐ ☐

Today's exercise

My Mood Today   ☹ ☹ ☺ ☺ ☺

Note

_____

_____

_____

_____

_____

A moment to remember

What I learnt today

Things that made me smile

Habits

Positive affirmation

Tomorrow's will

Date : _____   Today's goal: _____
Wake up time : _____   _____
Hours of sleep : _____   _____
        _____

What am I gratful for today	To do list

Meals

Breakfast	Lunch	Dinner	Snacks
Kcal	Kcal	Kcal	Kcal

Water intake	⊔ ⊔ ⊔ ⊔ ⊔ ⊔ ⊔ ⊔ ⊔ ⊔

Today's exercise

My Mood Today   ☹ 🙁 😐 🙂 😃

Note

_____
_____
_____
_____
_____

A moment to remember

What I learnt today

Things that made me smile

Habits

Positive affirmation

Tomorrow's will

Date : _____ Today's goal: _____

Wake up time : _____ _____

Hours of sleep : _____ _____

_____

What am I gratful for today	To do list

Meals

Breakfast	Lunch	Dinner	Snacks
Kcal	Kcal	Kcal	Kcal

Water intake	🥤 🥤 🥤 🥤 🥤 🥤 🥤 🥤 🥤 🥤

Today's exercise

My Mood Today   ☹ 🙁 🙂 😊 😄

Note

_____

_____

_____

_____

_____

A moment to remember

What I learnt today

Things that made me smile

Habits

Positive affirmation

Tomorrow's will

Date : _____   Today's goal: _____
Wake up time : _____   _____
Hours of sleep : _____   _____
_____

What am I gratful for today	To do list

Meals

Breakfast	Lunch	Dinner	Snacks
Kcal	Kcal	Kcal	Kcal

Water intake

Today's exercise

My Mood Today

Note

_____
_____
_____
_____

A moment to remember

What I learnt today

Things that made me smile

Habits

Positive affirmation

Tomorrow's will

Date : _____   Today's goal: _____

Wake up time : _____   _____

Hours of sleep : _____   _____

What am I gratful for today	To do list

Meals

Breakfast	Lunch	Dinner	Snacks
Kcal	Kcal	Kcal	Kcal

Water intake

Today's exercise

My Mood Today   😠 😟 😊 🙂 😃

Note

_____

_____

_____

_____

_____

A moment to remember

What I learnt today

Things that made me smile

Habits

Positive affirmation

Tomorrow's will

Date : _____   Today's goal: _____

Wake up time : _____   _____

Hours of sleep : _____   _____

What am I gratful for today	To do list

Meals

Breakfast	Lunch	Dinner	Snacks
Kcal	Kcal	Kcal	Kcal

Water intake ☐ ☐ ☐ ☐ ☐ ☐ ☐ ☐ ☐ ☐

Today's exercise

My Mood Today   ☹ 🙁 🙂 😊 😃

Note

_____
_____
_____
_____

A moment to remember

What I learnt today

Things that made me smile

Habits

Positive affirmation

Tomorrow's will

Date   : _____   Today's goal: _____
Wake up time : _____   _____
Hours of sleep : _____   _____
                                                    _____

What am I gratful for today	To do list

Meals

Breakfast	Lunch	Dinner	Snacks
Kcal	Kcal	Kcal	Kcal

Water intake	🥛 🥛 🥛 🥛 🥛 🥛 🥛 🥛 🥛 🥛

Today's exercise

My Mood Today   ☹ 🙁 🙂 😊 😃

Note

_____
_____
_____
_____
_____

A moment to remember

What I learnt today

Things that made me smile

Habits

Positive affirmation

Tomorrow's will

Date : _____ Today's goal: _____

Wake up time : _____ _____

Hours of sleep : _____ _____

_____

What am I gratful for today	To do list

Meals

Breakfast	Lunch	Dinner	Snacks
Kcal	Kcal	Kcal	Kcal

Water intake [ ] [ ] [ ] [ ] [ ] [ ] [ ] [ ] [ ] [ ]

Today's exercise

My Mood Today ☹ ☹ ☺ ☺ ☺

Note

_____
_____
_____
_____
_____

A moment to remember

What I learnt today

Things that made me smile

Habits

Positive affirmation

Tomorrow's will

Date   : _____   Today's goal: _____

Wake up time : _____   _____

Hours of sleep : _____   _____

_____

What am I gratful for today	To do list

Meals

Breakfast	Lunch	Dinner	Snacks
Kcal	Kcal	Kcal	Kcal

Water intake	🥛 🥛 🥛 🥛 🥛 🥛 🥛 🥛 🥛 🥛

Today's exercise

My Mood Today   😠 🙁 🙂 😊 😃

Note

_____

_____

_____

_____

A moment to remember

What I learnt today

Things that made me smile

Habits

Positive affirmation

Tomorrow's will

Date : _____   Today's goal: _____

Wake up time : _____   _____

Hours of sleep : _____   _____

_____

What am I gratful for today	To do list

Meals

Breakfast	Lunch	Dinner	Snacks
Kcal	Kcal	Kcal	Kcal

Water intake   🥛 🥛 🥛 🥛 🥛 🥛 🥛 🥛 🥛 🥛

Today's exercise

My Mood Today   😠 😟 🙂 😊 😃

Note

_____
_____
_____
_____

A moment to remember

What I learnt today

Things that made me smile

Positive affirmation

Habits

Tomorrow's will

Date : _____   Today's goal: _____

Wake up time : _____   _____

Hours of sleep : _____   _____

_____

What am I gratful for today	To do list

Meals

Breakfast	Lunch	Dinner	Snacks
Kcal	Kcal	Kcal	Kcal

Water intake   ▢ ▢ ▢ ▢ ▢ ▢ ▢ ▢ ▢ ▢

Today's exercise

My Mood Today   ☹ 🙁 🙂 😊 😃

Note

_____

_____

_____

_____

A moment to remember

What I learnt today

Things that made me smile

Habits

Positive affirmation

Tomorrow's will

Date : _____ Today's goal: _____

Wake up time : _____ _____

Hours of sleep : _____ _____

_____

What am I gratful for today	To do list

Meals

Breakfast	Lunch	Dinner	Snacks
Kcal	Kcal	Kcal	Kcal

Water intake ☐ ☐ ☐ ☐ ☐ ☐ ☐ ☐ ☐ ☐

Today's exercise

My Mood Today   ☹ 🙁 🙂 😊 😃

Note

_____
_____
_____
_____
_____

A moment to remember

What I learnt today

Things that made me smile

Habits

Positive affirmation

Tomorrow's will

Date : _____   Today's goal: _____
Wake up time : _____   _____
Hours of sleep : _____   _____

What am I gratful for today	To do list

Meals

Breakfast	Lunch	Dinner	Snacks
Kcal	Kcal	Kcal	Kcal
Water intake	🥛 🥛 🥛 🥛 🥛 🥛 🥛 🥛 🥛 🥛		

Today's exercise

My Mood Today   ☹ 🙁 🙂 😊 😄

Note

_____
_____
_____
_____
_____

A moment to remember

What I learnt today

Things that made me smile

Habits

Positive affirmation

Tomorrow's will

Date : _____   Today's goal: _____
Wake up time : _____   _____
Hours of sleep : _____   _____
_____

What am I gratful for today	To do list

Meals

Breakfast	Lunch	Dinner	Snacks
Kcal	Kcal	Kcal	Kcal

Water intake	🥛 🥛 🥛 🥛 🥛 🥛 🥛 🥛 🥛 🥛

Today's exercise

My Mood Today   😣 😟 🙂 😊 😃

Note
_____
_____
_____
_____
_____

A moment to remember

What I learnt today

Things that made me smile

Habits

Positive affirmation

Tomorrow's will

Date : _____   Today's goal: _____

Wake up time : _____   _____

Hours of sleep : _____   _____

_____

What am I gratful for today	To do list

Meals

Breakfast	Lunch	Dinner	Snacks
Kcal	Kcal	Kcal	Kcal

Water intake 🥛 🥛 🥛 🥛 🥛 🥛 🥛 🥛 🥛 🥛

Today's exercise

My Mood Today   ☹️ 🙁 🙂 😊 😃

Note

_____

_____

_____

_____

_____

A moment to remember

What I learnt today

Things that made me smile

Habits

Positive affirmation

Tomorrow's will

Date : _____   Today's goal: _____

Wake up time : _____   _____

Hours of sleep : _____   _____

What am I gratful for today	To do list

Meals

Breakfast	Lunch	Dinner	Snacks
Kcal	Kcal	Kcal	Kcal

Water intake	🥛 🥛 🥛 🥛 🥛 🥛 🥛 🥛 🥛 🥛

Today's exercise

My Mood Today   ☹ 🙁 🙂 😊 😀

Note

_____
_____
_____
_____
_____

A moment to remember

What I learnt today

Things that made me smile

Habits

Positive affirmation

Tomorrow's will

Date : _____   Today's goal: _____

Wake up time : _____   _____

Hours of sleep : _____   _____

What am I gratful for today	To do list

Meals

Breakfast	Lunch	Dinner	Snacks
Kcal	Kcal	Kcal	Kcal

Water intake

Today's exercise

My Mood Today   ☹ ☹ ☺ ☺ 😀

Note

_____

_____

_____

_____

A moment to remember

What I learnt today

Things that made me smile

Habits

Positive affirmation

Tomorrow's will

Date : _____   Today's goal: _____

Wake up time : _____   _____

Hours of sleep : _____   _____

_____

What am I gratful for today	To do list

Meals

Breakfast	Lunch	Dinner	Snacks
Kcal	Kcal	Kcal	Kcal

Water intake

Today's exercise

My Mood Today   ☹ ☹ ☺ ☺ ☺

Note

_____
_____
_____
_____
_____

A moment to remember

What I learnt today

Things that made me smile

Habits

Positive affirmation

Tomorrow's will

Date : _____

Wake up time : _____

Hours of sleep : _____

Today's goal: _____

_____

_____

What am I gratful for today	To do list

Meals

Breakfast	Lunch	Dinner	Snacks
Kcal	Kcal	Kcal	Kcal
Water intake			

Today's exercise

My Mood Today ☹ 🙁 🙂 😊 😃

Note

_____

_____

_____

_____

A moment to remember

What I learnt today

Things that made me smile

Habits

Positive affirmation

Tomorrow's will

Date : _____ Today's goal: _____

Wake up time : _____ _____

Hours of sleep : _____ _____

_____

What am I gratful for today

To do list

Meals

Breakfast	Lunch	Dinner	Snacks
Kcal	Kcal	Kcal	Kcal

Water intake ☐ ☐ ☐ ☐ ☐ ☐ ☐ ☐ ☐ ☐

Today's exercise

My Mood Today ☹ ☹ ☺ ☺ ☺

Note

_____

_____

_____

_____

A moment to remember

What I learnt today

Things that made me smile

Habits

Positive affirmation

Tomorrow's will

Date : _____   Today's goal: _____
Wake up time : _____   _____
Hours of sleep : _____   _____
                                     _____

What am I gratful for today	To do list

Meals

Breakfast	Lunch	Dinner	Snacks
Kcal	Kcal	Kcal	Kcal

Water intake

Today's exercise

My Mood Today

Note

_____
_____
_____
_____
_____

A moment to remember

What I learnt today

Things that made me smile

Habits

Positive affirmation

Tomorrow's will

Date : _____   Today's goal: _____

Wake up time : _____   _____

Hours of sleep : _____   _____

_____

What am I gratful for today	To do list

Meals

Breakfast	Lunch	Dinner	Snacks
Kcal	Kcal	Kcal	Kcal

Water intake	🥛 🥛 🥛 🥛 🥛 🥛 🥛 🥛 🥛 🥛

Today's exercise

My Mood Today   ☹ 🙁 🙂 😊 😀

Note

_____

_____

_____

_____

A moment to remember

What I learnt today

Things that made me smile

Habits

Positive affirmation

Tomorrow's will

Date   : _____   Today's goal: _____

Wake up time : _____   _____

Hours of sleep : _____   _____

What am I gratful for today	To do list

Meals

Breakfast	Lunch	Dinner	Snacks
Kcal	Kcal	Kcal	Kcal

Water intake

Today's exercise

My Mood Today   ☹ 🙁 🙂 😊 😄

Note

_____
_____
_____
_____
_____

A moment to remember

What I learnt today

Things that made me smile

Habits

Positive affirmation

Tomorrow's will

Date : _____   Today's goal: _____

Wake up time : _____   _____

Hours of sleep : _____   _____

_____

What am I gratful for today	To do list

Meals

Breakfast	Lunch	Dinner	Snacks
Kcal	Kcal	Kcal	Kcal

Water intake

Today's exercise

My Mood Today   ☹ ☹ ☺ ☺ ☺

Note

_____

_____

_____

_____

_____

A moment to remember

What I learnt today

Things that made me smile

Habits

Positive affirmation

Tomorrow's will

Date : _____   Today's goal: _____

Wake up time : _____   _____

Hours of sleep : _____   _____

_____

What am I gratful for today	To do list

Meals

Breakfast	Lunch	Dinner	Snacks
Kcal	Kcal	Kcal	Kcal

Water intake   🥛 🥛 🥛 🥛 🥛 🥛 🥛 🥛 🥛 🥛

Today's exercise

My Mood Today   ☹️ 🙁 🙂 😊 😀

Note

_____
_____
_____
_____
_____

A moment to remember

What I learnt today

Things that made me smile

Habits

Positive affirmation

Tomorrow's will

Date   : _____   Today's goal: _____

Wake up time : _____   _____

Hours of sleep : _____   _____

_____

What am I gratful for today	To do list

Meals

Breakfast	Lunch	Dinner	Snacks
Kcal	Kcal	Kcal	Kcal

Water intake   🥛 🥛 🥛 🥛 🥛 🥛 🥛 🥛 🥛 🥛

Today's exercise

My Mood Today   ☹ 🙁 🙂 😊 😃

Note

_____

_____

_____

_____

A moment to remember

What I learnt today

Things that made me smile

Habits

Positive affirmation

Tomorrow's will

Date   : _____   Today's goal: _____

Wake up time : _____   _____

Hours of sleep : _____   _____

_____

What am I gratful for today	To do list

Meals

Breakfast	Lunch	Dinner	Snacks
Kcal	Kcal	Kcal	Kcal

| Water intake | | | | | | | | | | | |

Today's exercise

My Mood Today   ☹ ☹ ☺ ☺ ☺

Note

_____

_____

_____

_____

_____

A moment to remember

What I learnt today

Things that made me smile

Habits

Positive affirmation

Tomorrow's will

Date : _____   Today's goal: _____

Wake up time : _____   _____

Hours of sleep : _____   _____

What am I gratful for today	To do list

Meals

Breakfast	Lunch	Dinner	Snacks
Kcal	Kcal	Kcal	Kcal
Water intake	🥛 🥛 🥛 🥛 🥛 🥛 🥛 🥛 🥛 🥛		

Today's exercise

My Mood Today   ☹ 🙁 😐 🙂 😃

Note

_____

_____

_____

_____

A moment to remember

What I learnt today

Things that made me smile

Habits

Positive affirmation

Tomorrow's will

Date   : _____   Today's goal: _____
Wake up time : _____   _____
Hours of sleep : _____   _____
                                     _____

What am I gratful for today	To do list

Meals

Breakfast	Lunch	Dinner	Snacks
Kcal	Kcal	Kcal	Kcal
Water intake	▯ ▯ ▯ ▯ ▯ ▯ ▯ ▯ ▯ ▯		

Today's exercise

My Mood Today   ☹ ☹ ☺ ☺ ☺

Note

_____
_____
_____
_____
_____

A moment to remember

What I learnt today

Things that made me smile

Habits

Positive affirmation

Tomorrow's will

Date : _____   Today's goal: _____

Wake up time : _____   _____

Hours of sleep : _____   _____

What am I gratful for today

To do list

Meals

Breakfast	Lunch	Dinner	Snacks
Kcal	Kcal	Kcal	Kcal

Water intake

Today's exercise

My Mood Today   ☹ 😕 🙂 😊 😃

Note

_____
_____
_____
_____

A moment to remember

What I learnt today

Things that made me smile

Habits

Positive affirmation

Tomorrow's will

Date : _____ Today's goal: _____

Wake up time : _____ _____

Hours of sleep : _____ _____

What am I gratful for today	To do list

Meals

Breakfast	Lunch	Dinner	Snacks
Kcal	Kcal	Kcal	Kcal

Water intake ☐ ☐ ☐ ☐ ☐ ☐ ☐ ☐ ☐ ☐

Today's exercise

My Mood Today ☹ ☹ 😐 ☺ 😄

Note

_____

_____

_____

_____

_____

A moment to remember

What I learnt today

Things that made me smile

Habits

Positive affirmation

Tomorrow's will

Date : _____   Today's goal: _____
Wake up time : _____   _____
Hours of sleep : _____   _____
_____

What am I gratful for today	To do list

Meals

Breakfast	Lunch	Dinner	Snacks
Kcal	Kcal	Kcal	Kcal

Water intake 🥛 🥛 🥛 🥛 🥛 🥛 🥛 🥛 🥛 🥛

Today's exercise

My Mood Today 😠 ☹️ 🙂 😊 😃

Note

_____
_____
_____
_____

A moment to remember

What I learnt today

Things that made me smile

Habits

Positive affirmation

Tomorrow's will

Date : _____ Today's goal: _____
Wake up time : _____ _____
Hours of sleep : _____ _____
_____

What am I gratful for today	To do list

Meals

Breakfast	Lunch	Dinner	Snacks
Kcal	Kcal	Kcal	Kcal

Water intake

Today's exercise

My Mood Today ☹ 🙁 😐 🙂 😃

Note

_____
_____
_____
_____
_____

A moment to remember

What I learnt today

Things that made me smile

Habits

Positive affirmation

Tomorrow's will

Date : _____   Today's goal: _____

Wake up time : _____   _____

Hours of sleep : _____   _____

_____

What am I gratful for today	To do list

Meals

Breakfast	Lunch	Dinner	Snacks
Kcal	Kcal	Kcal	Kcal

Water intake	☐ ☐ ☐ ☐ ☐ ☐ ☐ ☐ ☐ ☐

Today's exercise

My Mood Today   😠 😞 😊 🙂 😃

Note

_____
_____
_____
_____

A moment to remember

What I learnt today

Things that made me smile

Habits

Positive affirmation

Tomorrow's will

Date   : _____   Today's goal: _____

Wake up time : _____   _____

Hours of sleep : _____   _____

What am I gratful for today	To do list

Meals

Breakfast	Lunch	Dinner	Snacks
Kcal	Kcal	Kcal	Kcal
Water intake			

Today's exercise

My Mood Today   ☹ 🙁 🙂 😊 😃

Note

_____
_____
_____
_____
_____

A moment to remember

What I learnt today

Things that made me smile

Habits

Positive affirmation

Tomorrow's will

Date : _____   Today's goal: _____
Wake up time : _____   _____
Hours of sleep : _____   _____
_____

What am I gratful for today	To do list

Meals

Breakfast	Lunch	Dinner	Snacks
Kcal	Kcal	Kcal	Kcal

Water intake ☐ ☐ ☐ ☐ ☐ ☐ ☐ ☐ ☐ ☐

Today's exercise

My Mood Today   ☹ ☹ ☺ ☺ ☺

Note

_____
_____
_____
_____
_____

A moment to remember

What I learnt today

Things that made me smile

Habits

Positive affirmation

Tomorrow's will

Made in the USA
Columbia, SC
24 March 2022

58077751R10096